INCARCERATED THINKING

by
Quinton Mostella

Copyright © 2023 Quinton Mostella

Book Package and Publication
Leadership DevelopME, LLC: www.leadershipdevelopme.com

Graphics & Book Cover Design: Wesley "Tune Bee" Barner
Artistic sketching on the original cover concept: Greg Mathis
Editor: Elana Curry

All rights reserved. No part of this book may be used or reproduced by any means, graphic, electronic, or mechanical, including photocopying, recording, taping, or by any information storage retrieval system without the written permission of the publisher except in the case of brief quotations embodied in critical articles and reviews.

Books may be ordered through booksellers or by contacting:

Quinton Mostella
Email: savedandsoldoutmin@gmail.com

Because of the dynamic nature of the Internet, any web addresses or links contained in this book may have changed since publication and may no longer be valid. The views expressed in this work are solely those of the author and do not necessarily reflect the views of the publisher, and the publisher hereby disclaims any responsibility for them.

Any people depicted in stock imagery provided by the Internet are being used for illustrative purposes only. *Incarcerated Thinking* is a work of nonfiction. Details in some letters have been changed to protect the identities of the persons involved.

ISBN: 978-1-365-58295-0
Library of Congress Control Number: 2023903322

Printed in the United States of America

Scripture taken from **The ESV Global Study Bible®**, ESV® Bible Copyright © 2012 by Crossway.
Scripture quotations are taken from the *Holy Bible*, **New Living Translation**, copyright ©1996, 2004, 2015 by Tyndale House Foundation.
Scripture taken from the **New King James Version®**. Copyright © 1982 by Thomas Nelson..
Scriptures taken from the Holy Bible, **New International Version®**, NIV®. Copyright © 1973, 1978, 1984, 2011 by Biblica, Inc.™

All rights reserved

Used by Permission

DEDICATION

This book is dedicated to all who are fighting to recapture the ultimate goal: Freedom. Despite your situation, you still can impact lives within your family, friends, community and your nation. Always remember that with God nothing shall be impossible...

Illustrator: Greg Mathis

"I have held many things in my hands, and I have lost them all, but whatever I have placed in God's hands, that I still possess."

- Martin Luther -

Illustrator: Greg Mathis

"Life isn't about finding yourself;
it's about creating yourself."

- *George Bernard Shaw* –

TABLE OF CONTENTS

Acknowledgments 1

Introduction 5

Topic 1: Desiring Companionship 6

Topic 2: The Longing 8

Topic 3: After Her Visit 10

Topic 4: Love Letter 13

Topic 5: Birthday Celebrations 15

Topic 6: Change 17

Topic 7: Surviving Maximum Security 19

Topic 8: Opportunity Dwells Amid Opposition 22

Topic 9: The Cycle 24

Topic 10: Explanation 28

Topic 11: The Giver 31

Topic 12: Can You Love Beyond Your Hurt? 34

Topic 13: Letter to My Mother 36

Topic 14:	How It Happened: A Retelling of a Friend's Account	39
Topic 15:	Misinformed	42
Topic 16:	Thinking Out Loud	45
Topic 17:	Thank You, Sister	47
Topic 18:	The Battle	49
Topic 19:	The Story of Chaos and Confusion	51
Topic 20:	Letter to a Friend	56
Topic 21:	I'm not a Product of Where I am	59
Topic 22:	Encouragement to a Female Friend	61
Topic 23:	Encouraging a Friend in Christ's Love	66
Topic 24:	A Special Thank You	69
Topic 25:	Letter to Mario	72
Topic 26:	Words of Encouragement	74
Topic 27:	The Clear-up	76
Topic 28:	Letter to My Brother	79
Topic 29:	Encouraging My Friend's Sister	82
Topic 30:	Appreciation for My Brother's Love	85
Topic 31:	A Letter to My Sons: Quintaveous and Quinzarius	88
Topic 32:	Appreciation of Your Generosity	91
Topic 33:	A Clear Letter	94

Topic 34:	I Apologize for Me	97
Topic 35:	Encouragement for My Niece	99
Topic 36:	How We Started	102
Topic 37:	The Resurrection of a Man	109
Topic 38:	Encouragement for Your Time of Need	111
Topic 39:	The Depth of My Environment	114
Topic 40:	My Reality	117
Topic 41:	Sometimes, I Wish I was Deaf	120
Topic 42:	Running	122
Topic 43:	Encouragement for My Brother	124
Topic 44:	Who You are in Christ	128
Topic 45:	From Loki to Quinton	131
Topic 46:	When I Found the Book	136
Topic 47:	To the Woman who Inspired Me	139
Conclusion		142
In Memory of...		144

ACKNOWLEDGMENTS

First and foremost, I want to thank my Lord and Savior, Jesus Christ, the King of kings and Lord of lords. I thank God for all the blessings, trials, and afflictions that helped produce the content of this glorious masterpiece.

I want to generally thank my family for their undeniable love and support, not just during my incarceration but my entire life. I want to thank everyone who ever sent a card, letter or even prayed for me. Thank you so much! I also want to thank all who have left me, betrayed me or just did not like me. You have helped push me into who I am today.

Thank you to my beautiful mother, Jackie Davis. Mama, you have been above and beyond what a mother should be. You never condemned, judged, or criticized any of my shortcomings: instead, you just simply loved me through it all. I am sorry for all the disappointments and embarrassments I put you through. I pray this puts a smile on your face, I love you mama.

Shawntae, I still remember when you told me to write this book, and I was like, "no way!" So thank you for seeing something in me that I didn't see in myself. I want to thank God for all the men and women of God who have ever ministered to me. I thank Will, my father in the faith, and Sister Coburn, my mother in the faith. I also want to thank my little brother Nikea who influenced my kids, who is always willing to invest in my dreams. To my children, Quintaveous, Quinzarius, Ma'Tejah and Quinzariya thank you all for respecting me. I love you all. And a huge thanks to my brother Aubrey, who has encouraged me and took time to type the pages you're reading. Thank God for him and his tireless efforts. Thank you, Tune Bee, for coming through for me. I really appreciate it. Despite the difficulty, we made it happen. Man, thank you, my guy G (Gregory Mathis) for bringing my thoughts into reality. I truly appreciate you.

Respectfully, I want to say thank you to 1B Pod Turney Center. All the brothers who helped me, inspired me, encouraged me and listened to me throughout my journey. Thank you. To my Joy Joy, my future, thank you for all you do for me. I know there were times when I may have asked you to copy this or call that person and you never hesitated. You were always looking out for me. Thank you for your insight, wisdom, love, and genuine care. I thank God the Father always for blessing me with a woman like you. I love you. Thank you.

I thank God for all the people He has used to inspire me and push me into my purpose. All the brothers and sisters, who have given me their ear to hear and given me constructive criticism. Thank you all and I hope that you are positively impacted by my *Incarcerated Thinking*.

INTRODUCTION

I have been given one purpose for writing this book: I aim to provide clarity and insight into the mind of a man incarcerated in the justice system. The public perception of incarcerated men and women has been distorted for centuries due to uninformed media outlets and various other propaganda. I want this body of work to change that.

This book will give you an intimate relationship with my thoughts over the full span of my incarceration. As you navigate through these writings, you will have a firsthand experience of a young male who transformed into a young man when he encountered Jesus Christ. Each chapter consists of personal letters or topics expressed from my thinking according to the situation, location and stage of development I was in at that moment. I would love for my story to spark a change in the common perception; however, my biggest desire is to provide a journey inside the mind of a man incarcerated. My desire is to increase your understanding.

DESIRING COMPANIONSHIP

MAXIMUM SECURITY, WEST HIGH PRISON

2011

Dear Latoya,

I hope you are doing well. I'm taking things day by day here with being on lockdown 23 hours per day and only having one day of recreation. Within these two years of incarceration, my heart has been wide open. Writing has been my main outlet.

Now, I have sincerely finalized who I am as a man. I mustered up the courage to say that I love you more than I have known love in my whole life. I miss you so much that deep thoughts of you send my mind into a trance. Lately, I have found myself replaying some of our past conversations. Conversations with you are like symphonies and sweet jazz to my ear. It's like you have some sort of untamable verbal passion that sends my mind to places I have never deemed imaginable.

How have you taken such control over my emotions? Baby, my longing is to experience life with you as a husband should his wife. My life desires to live for you. Have you ever taken the time to realize that I grew to love you from the inside out? Initially, it was your outward beauty that (physically) attracted me to you, but your inner essence is what made me fall in love with you. Always remember: you are my sanctuary, and no dictionary has the words to explain all that you have truly meant to my life. I love you, and I wrote this short missive while waiting for yours to arrive. To allow you to feel even more of how much I truly and wholeheartedly love you.

THE LONGING

WEST HIGH PRISON, MAXIMUM SECURITY
2011

Dear Joslyn, my companion,

Usually, after receiving a card from you – a card filled with such warmth – I would instantly begin to convey all that is on my heart. Unfortunately, on this occasion, I was halted by the desire to ensure that you genuinely understood the depths of my feelings toward you. A few perspectives need to be assessed by both of us as we proceed as companions.

I love you beyond humanity, and there is nothing more that I want than for our hearts to be equivalent to each other. Have you ever been in a relationship and had to pretend not to love your significant other as much? Would you do it to prove how much they loved you? It's strange, I know, but relevant to how I feel at times. Looking at the pictures you sent me, I am astounded by your beauty, and

I am sure other guys are as well. But I do not want my feelings to be hindered by the things I have no control over.

Open up to me. Explain how you feel and reiterate to me that what we have is not void. I admit I am vulnerable and lonely right now. I've never been this alone in my life. But the questions I have for you are still valid. So please open up to me.

AFTER HER VISIT

TURNEY CENTER ANNEX, WAYNE COUNTY
2014

Michelle, my heart,

Before I begin to scribble my thoughts upon this heartfelt passage, I must continue to thank God for His amazing grace and for keeping a beautiful, smart, talented, God-fearing woman like yourself in my life throughout these years. Words cannot express nor explain how much of a blessing you truly are and have always been.

Lately, it has been back to the basics. I've been exploring the Bible to equip myself with the proper awareness to overcome all the daily obstacles during this process of shaping myself into who God wants me to become. I would be telling you a story if I said that I did not have weaknesses because every man and woman living on this earth has weaknesses. However, I am learning daily that God will present certain situations to actually confirm the growth that my lips have expressed. He'll surround you with individuals who may be a headache to a degree, only to affirm that you have truly humbled yourself when you don't lash out or get disgruntled; rather, you let those individuals do what they do and not let them consume your energy or time.

So by being in this kind of environment, one has to always remain focused on what is most important, relying on a higher power to provide that guidance and wisdom, which will become your third eye to see the future. Nevertheless, one must always stay mindful of the blessings bestowed upon him. In this case, it's having the opportunity and the pleasure to converse with you through these letters. Not to mention gazing into your lovely eyes while admiring those dimples accompanied by your beautiful smile, which brought about an overwhelmingly internal eruption. This was compounded by the authenticity of you providing such concern in my perpetual struggle, which is so very rare amongst most young women. I refuse to mislead, misinform or misguide you in any way. That would hinder the nourishment of a friendship once damaged by my selfish ways. I thank God, despite my immaturity and all my foolishness, that He kept you in my life. Conversing with a woman like you made me expand my mind so that the probability of acquiring and achieving more is in contrast to all your accomplishments.

Lord knows I hated to see you leave, but I enjoyed watching motionless as you smiled and waved goodbye, which put the exclamation point on my whole day. Tell your sister I appreciate her concern. I am doing just fine. Just continue to strive – excel in all your endeavors. With God on your side, nothing is impossible. With that being said, a confirmation of this letter from my heart to yours would be tremendously appreciated.

LOVE LETTER

WAYNE COUNTY ANNEX
2016

Dear Joslyn, my companion,

With persistent endurance, accompanied by loyal longevity and a balanced chain of communication, I have often found myself rationalizing the thought of *where did we go wrong?* The companionship between us went way beyond our expectations of brilliant love; however, my immaturity led me to believe in the quantity of women I must be involved with rather than appreciating the quality of the woman I was truly in love with. Therefore, I write you now not to return to a romantic relationship but to own up to my faults.

All the turmoil and chaos with the reality of your departure has ruined me beyond all belief. Of course, there are no instruction manuals for interrupting relationships, but the consistent conversation could have helped us establish a more secure foundation. At times, I was honestly flattered by the attention of sexy women, which led me to be tempted by the opportunity. It all resulted in engaging in sexual immorality.

Being without you has made me cherish what could have been. The ongoing reminders of how good we were together overwhelmed my soul. I feel as if I neglected my duties of being the protector, the soul provider, and the overseer of our relationship. But because of the extended amount of time we have spent semi-separated from one another, it has brought about a mental and emotional awakening that has cured me.

I ask that you not let the ashes of the past supersede the spark that could ignite a fire of passion lasting longer than a one-night experience. My growth over the course of these past years is my revived outlook on seeing life from a different perspective. I also hope that my continued advancement would at least earn the just reward of us chancing this once again. So, as I end, when your time permits, a confirmation of this paradox from my heart to yours would be tremendously appreciated!

BIRTHDAY CELEBRATIONS

WAYNE COUNTY ANNEX
2016

To Whom It May Concern,

Humbly speaking, birthdays are days no person living on this beautiful earth will ever forget. Meanwhile, over time we as a black nation have slowly glorified the celebration of our birthdays through the consumption of irresponsible drinking or the overuse of drugs, neither of which reflects the sole purpose of our true being. On the contrary, it opposes the significance of birth in which God placed us here for His divine purpose. Take into consideration that I, too, have fallen victim to these types of celebrations; however, there comes a time in life that calls for total refocusing mentally and spiritually. It will cause an abrupt change in your thinking, which will ultimately transcend the old pattern of thought to a more mature, responsible approach to handling and appreciating this glorious day that you were blessed to have on this earth.

My words are brief but filled with exuberant energy, hoping against hope that you would consider correction before criticism. With that said, may you swim in the ocean of abundance, manifesting your own divine destiny!

CHANGE

WAYNE COUNTY ANNEX

2016

Journal Entry

When a person limits themselves to a certain group of people, how can we expect them to think on a higher level than what they have become accustomed to? For instance, a person can only identify with what they have seen, heard, or read. If the mind is not constantly being fed its proper ingredients so that a person can progress to become more productive, they will eventually repeat the same cycle of behavior. Their train of thought has not been corrected in order to break the cycle. This has been my story, even today, while still affiliated with GD.

So when an individual strives tirelessly to resurrect themselves, they will then be able to participate in communication with their significant other on various topics. Despite the tension, neither one will become repugnant by the different perspectives of their partner. And by doing so, the chemistry will be established so they will be able to converse well, finding common ground to compel one another towards their goals.

People are going to change. Your health is going to change. Finances change. The one constant in life is the idea of change. The point I am trying to make is that for you to change your life, you must change your mindset. Whenever a person changes their mindset, they can become more than what they have settled for. For example, suppose a homeless man alters how he thinks about being homeless and adopts a prosperity mindset accompanied by action. In that case, he will soon rise up from his state of poverty. In the Bible, Romans 12:2 says, "And do not be conformed to this world, but be transformed by the renewing of your mind." So, I challenge you to not let your mind become the bench of relaxation and stagnation but to allow it to be your compass guiding you from one dimension of your life to the next. This will help as you diligently strive to maximize all of your God-given gifts to their full capacity. Never let your dreams of tomorrow be hindered by the mindset that you possess today.

SURVIVING MAXIMUM SECURITY

WAYNE COUNTY ANNEX
2016

To Whom It May Concern,

I want to ask you a question. Have you ever found yourself in a situation or a place that was in total contradiction to the normalcy you have been accustomed to? If you may, allow me to capture a second of your time so that I can paint a picture of my experience in maximum security prison.

It has been 4 years since leaving maximum security. Still, I vividly remember often talking to myself to maintain my sanity due to the enormous amount of strain maximum security could place on one's mental state by being confined to a cell 23 hours a day. But my insurmountable measure of integrity and dignity would not allow me to masturbate in the sight of a woman nor throw my urine on an officer or inmate as others regularly did. That would be in total disagreement with who I was as a person.

I understand that the concept of adversity can seem simplistic, but it is rather complex overall. Without mutual love for the outside world, one tends to submit to the prison lifestyle and form a redundant bond with prison companionship by accepting defeat.

Never could I fathom the thought of being a participant in maximum security; nevertheless, I was placed in it based on the vital mistakes that I had made. Despite all the excessive amount of noise and distractions, I read for countless hours daily. My attitude of becoming greater trumped the attitude of my environment of settling for the lesser. The more I read, the more my mind began to transform. Therefore, I started to use my imagination to create images of me being involved with family, kids, friends, and women. Even adventurous trips, which ultimately caused me to understand the freedom of thought, permitted me to enjoy the society's luxury and still be confined to a cell.

This strategic form of thinking mixed with daily exercise helped keep my physical, mental, and spiritual health aligned with my goal of becoming more intellectually and spiritually sound. I challenged myself to reach within to discover the hidden gifts. I also reminded myself of the ultimate goal of never yielding to the characteristics of maximum security. (Statistics say that type of environment causes the demoralization of the mind.) Instead, I humbly and gracefully resurrected my entire being, overtaking what was supposed to defeat me, and reincarnated a believer who was destined to shape himself in the image of the One he was created from. Without Jesus and His word, I would not have survived (Romans 8:18).

OPPORTUNITY DWELLS AMID OPPOSITION

WAYNE COUNTY ANNEX
2016

Journal Entry

From the perspective of some, opposition and opportunity are equivalent to each other. Opposition can be defined by hardships, financial instability, sickness, and incarceration. In contrast, opportunity is associated with such things as promotion, power, and wealth coming from a poverty state of thinking to an abundant state of maturity. The question could be raised of how two words with opposite effects of good and bad, or negative and positive, could even exist in the same realm. Again, it surely rests upon how one perceives the two.

A lot of times, people in this day and age who lack spiritual maturity and self-awareness stare in the face of opposition and feel defeated. They allow the pressure of that opposition or event to consume them to the point that their mind fixates on what happened as opposed to thinking, *What am I going to make happen despite what has happened?* Opportunity lies in the depth of opposition only to be received by the tireless Godly thoughts produced in one's mind through a continual transformation. The transformation comes through erasing worldly thoughts that form how you feel about the lead director to how you view a situation by equipping yourself with the wisdom of God to identify the advancement that will arise despite your crisis rather than letting your mind become stagnant focusing solely on the crisis itself.

My point is that you must permit your opposition in life to be conducive to the acceleration of your opportunity only by negating the discouragement and discomfort of the process so that you can be impelled to obtain your promise. As my thoughts begin to disappear from this glorious passage, may you not wither in the woods of discomfort but excel in the forest of prosperity.

THE CYCLE

WAYNE COUNTY ANNEX
2016

Journal Entry

Normally I would begin writing solely being led by the spirit. On this occasion, I was halted by the deep desire to elaborate on a cycle that has significant ramifications on the lives of young black men. There's a terrible cycle occurring that must change.

Sometimes in life, we must stop and think before we pass judgment on the actions of others instead of criticizing - condemnation being the result of our thinking. So, why don't we ever ask why people do some of the things that they do?

For example, Tony, a young, vibrant boy growing up in a crime-infested and impoverished neighborhood surrounded by family members whose employment is one of illegal activity that proves to provide a lifestyle of luxurious cars, exotic women, and the absence of a father's influence and guidance has Tony's future of college in question at a young age. While searching for an identity and love from a male figure, Tony has become intrigued and infatuated with the lifestyle of selling drugs because it is all he sees when he exits his door, along with friends making money providing for themselves.

Now John is like a big brother/father figure that Tony has always longed for, and John looks out for Tony the same way another male looked out for him by supplying Tony with drugs. (He secretly refuses to watch him work for someone else.) You see, the correlation that exists between the two is that they both have been misguided. While John is only doing what he has been taught, Tony's vulnerability and the void of a male figure needing acceptance allow him not to see clearly. He's thinking only about instant gratification rather than working or going to school for delayed gratification. Tony has now acquired a level of arrogance and obnoxiousness intoxicated from the success of making money, so much so that he has now become oblivious to his immature behavior. He does not know that he is drawing unwanted attention from law enforcement that could be very detrimental to the entire existence he has ever known.

After turning eighteen, Tony is indicted on four counts of the sale of cocaine in the midst of having 14 grams of cocaine in his possession upon his arrest. How many of you think John has impacted how Tony's life could have turned out? How many of you think he is the sole reason Tony is facing 15 years at 100% and in a world of discomfort with a future of uncertainty? This cycle happens too often in our communities across the U.S. It is not by cruel intentions but by misguidance. John was only doing what he was taught. John does not know his influence, and his choice to provide the drugs has caused great destruction to another black family. Without a father's presence and strong family support, Tony found himself depicting the characteristics of what he was longing for from John that impacted the decision he made, landing him in prison for the next 15 years of his life. This is the cycle that continues to plague our community today.

It is now time for us as grown black men to set an example while being an example for our youth to model so that their future consists of prosperity and hope. To ignite a future generation to be innovators, engineers, world leaders, and world changers. To maximize all the gifts God has provided for them, rather than settling for street corners and jail cells. They are becoming another statistic in a systemic cycle of incarceration that every 1 out of 3 families is familiar with.

EXPLANATION

WAYNE COUNTY ANNEX
2016

Dear Joslyn, my companion,

After thoroughly examining your missive, I was astonished by the depth of the language you expressed concerning how you have been feeling about us. More often than not, when I receive a letter from you, I would instantly begin to convey everything on my heart; however, on this particular occasion, I was halted by the desire to listen with my mind rather than read with my heart.

In my book, I have a chapter called *Change*. I personally think change is the most fluctuation that life has to offer because if you are ill-prepared to adapt to your transformation, then you will lose out on the significance of rejoicing. You'll remain stagnate because of how you perceive a process of change.

Eight years have passed since God has transformed my level of thinking for a standard of an attitude I strive tirelessly to possess. I hope to imitate the attributes of Christ by remaining humble and transparent in the shadow of any difficulties that may arise. I am searching endlessly for positivity despite the circumstances, but you were absent for the entirety of that transition process. So, you must understand why the complexity lies between how you feel about me and differs from how I feel about you. It is due to the extensive amount of time we separated without continuous conversing that didn't exist between us.

For example, let's say an individual drives a 2010 Malibu and is also purchasing a 2016 GMC Sierra truck. He can't receive the same performance from the Sierra as he would from the Malibu. This is because one is a car, and one is a truck. The Sierra is bigger, so the capacity to have more space and endure more inclement weather is beyond the limitation that exists with the Malibu. Plus, the truck is newer, so he would have to learn how to drive and use all the new technology that comes with it.

As it relates to me, I am the Sierra that one knows nothing about, so it would be highly unlikely for me to manufacture old feelings operating from this new machine (body) that would not be in harmony with the mindset I now possess. Without insight into how I think or having any idea of the total transformation I endured, there will be limited understanding of my changed behavior. Therefore, that limited understanding will lead to us being out of sync because of a lack of substance, causing the relationship to end.

For anyone to go with me, they must grow with me, or they will drown trying to follow me to my destiny. Therefore, it is imperative that they understand who I am now.

THE GIVER

WAYNE COUNTY ANNEX
2016

Journal Entry

Has there ever been a time or times in your life when you felt depleted mentally and emotionally from providing an insurmountable amount of energy for a person that is unwilling to progress? What about remaining in the mess because of the people who accompany the one in the midst of the mess? For example, have you ever found yourself engaging with an individual about altering their thoughts for the attainment of a better circumstance, but you soon come to realize that the individual is content possessing a mediocre mind? They avoid maximizing their full potential because they don't want to put in the hard work.

When someone like me is a giver of not just money but love, time, and resources, they must be extremely cautious. Without limitations on how much they give or who they choose to give to, the giver can become blinded by the relationship. But without equal energy reciprocated back to the giver, it will eventually drain them. This is due to the amount of energy that has been remitted into the other without replenishing from the counterpart.

No matter how bad you want success (not just financial) for someone, they must want success for themselves too. If not, you will find yourself weary because of your inability to accept that the mindset you desire for the other person can only be rectified through a process of evolution that does not involve you. It is rarely about the power one taps into, but the pain one disconnects from. That is what ultimately permits the vision to see beyond the hindrance they continue to place upon themself due to the lack of self-awareness that they refuse to correct. What they may stumble upon would be more confusing and complex to remove. Instead of the convenience and comfort of remaining in the field with the swine, they are supposed to be eating in the palace.

While I write this to vent about my fatigue of constantly giving, I also write as a desperate plea to God, asking that He bring someone who could pour into me just as I've poured into others.

CAN YOU LOVE BEYOND YOUR HURT?

WAYNE COUNTY ANNEX
2016

Dear Hurt Woman,

Whenever a man has caused a lot of hurt, exhaustion, and lonely nights for his woman during his stage of personal development and self-discovery, her wounds may not rehabilitate as she says they do. She'll misuse words to bandage her true feelings, but that causes him to misunderstand. And he is only seeking to rediscover himself despite his past mistakes so that he can finally become the man she was longing for. But for them to even sustain a healthy, loving, and trustworthy relationship, she has to be totally honest about her insecurities that so often are masked by a smile. Internally, that smile is connected to a heart-wrenching howl that no one seems to identify. It is the hurdle to be jumped.

As the man embarks upon the journey of redemption, which occurs through endless correction and allowing his behavior to align with his language, it can become increasingly frustrating not to receive acknowledgments from his woman for his tireless efforts of overcoming the issue, which ignites her insecurity from the beginning. Despite his past transgression, he refuses to be mistreated or misunderstood in any way that may halt his growth and development. So, it's strictly about this woman taking the time out of time, removing him from what he did while replacing him for who he is becoming. In this way, she can actually observe the progression of honesty and sincerity in his words while evaluating his performance amid their reality, still withholding the possibility of envisioning a future together. All he asks of his woman is total forgiveness and acceptance of what still can be without using his past mistakes as a weapon against him whenever she feels the same way she felt prior to his transgression.

So, my question to you, dear woman, is whether it's possible for you to love *me* beyond your hurt or remain in the field of uncertainty, giving up on what could be all because of how you perceive he should be?

LETTER TO MY MOTHER

TURNEY COUNTY ANNEX,
MAXIMUM SECURITY
2016

Dear Mom,

I'm thinking about you today. Trying to navigate my way through these muddy waters, but somehow, regardless of my tireless efforts, I seem to never prevail. I'm constantly pondering on a variety of avenues to escape. My decisions hindered me from walking out of the consequences of my past, yet I never lost sight of the promises of my future. Wrestling with my thoughts, I was reminded of a few things that pointed me to one person.

Exposure is the key to one's state of attainment, whether it's a material possession or knowledge. Despite overwhelming challenges, what I witnessed as a child and through my adolescence was the observation of unexplainable strength. It was accompanied by a tenacious attitude while being a single black mother of three, surrounded by people in a ghetto with big dreams but low expectations. They were comfortable with where they were as opposed to where they could be. You displayed a level of determination and progression to maximize all of your potential. You wanted to achieve the goals in which you set out to accomplish. That has been engraved upon my spirit years later, teaching me that regardless of severe hardships, the mental capacity one must possess in order to withstand any stronghold one is up against is a true testament to their character, which is an attribute I now possess. It has permitted me to stand in the face of adversity beyond one's imagination, never becoming bushed or unresolved but staying exuberant and persistent to maximize the possibilities of my situation rather than letting my situation mute who I am and define who I will become. The gathering of information is not to belittle or look down upon but to enlighten, empower and awaken all my people who are still asleep in the middle of the day. This is my sole intention, so the cycle of destruction is not repeated due to the lack of conscience one does not possess. Mama, I finally reached out to God when the acid of my pain destroyed the wall of my desire.

HOW IT HAPPENED: A RETELLING OF A FRIEND'S ACCOUNT

WAYNE COUNTY ANNEX

2017

Dear Anonymous,

After all that we have invested in one another, the thought of us departing never crossed our minds. In times of adversity, our love for one another never wavered nor showed any implication of moving in the opposite direction until the day someone was apprehended for a vital mistake that changed the dynamics of not only our lives but our relationship forever. Being optimistic about the journey ahead as it relates to the incarceration process seemed a little easier knowing I have a partner indebted in my struggle that would ultimately make the transition from one dimension to the next a little smoother.

The adjustment to the loneliness, compounded with the strain of confusion, can cause a person's attention to become altered by the overwhelming number of voices repeatedly saying move on. As time progresses, the responsibilities continue to mount, causing stress levels to increase. This increases one's attitude to that of absurdity because the comfort of one's voice, touch, and presence remain absent in the midst of her vulnerability reaching its maximum capacity to the point that she is longing to fulfill the void she is so accustomed to. Without any cruel intent, she begins to interact with mediocre people, increasing her involvement in people who were non-existent prior to his incarceration. This is due to the misguidance of what is feeding her desires, which often leads her into a situation resulting in lifelong consequences of a moment of pleasure. Nevertheless, if she is entangled with a stubborn, controlling, argumentative man whose incarceration has clouded his vision, it ignites a hidden insecurity stemming from the uncertainty that can intoxicate his curiosity, which is already on the brink of total manifestation. Consistent conversing between the two is still the primary focus of maintaining the relationship, but the overall tone of concern and affection for one's being has significantly differed from how it was in the beginning.

Noticing this drastic change, the lust for infidelity continues to scratch the surface of one's mind. But it does not grasp the soul of the amount of depth attached to the sacrifices and struggles over the years. Whenever an individual has forecasted a specific type of weather sketch in his mind fitting for an easy ending, what he has cultivated prematurely can severely affect a person's reality that holds no significant value to what is actually taking place outside the bubble mind he refuses to remove himself from. Simultaneously, the day approached where the reality he made up in his mind clashes with reality which is in total contrast with one another, leading to the unveiling of sexual misbehavior on his woman's behalf that leaves him in a state of astonishment and hurt, causing a separation of the two people with history, all from one person's mistake. Always be conscious of the decisions you make because you will not be the only one affected in the process.

MISINFORMED

TURNEY COUNTY ANNEX
2017

Journal Entry

I'm close to going home after being indicted for first-degree murder. I'm perplexed by the rumors and opinions surrounding me, and I need to write to release my emotions instead of resorting to negative behavior and words. Therefore, as circumstances arise in our life that correlates to the lifestyle we're used to living, it will cause those around us to question, doubt, and be in disagreement with our choices. For example, if all the mistakes you have ever made became public, then the opportunity for people to criticize increases because the vital information that was once a theory has now become the subject of criticism.

There seems as though there is an ideology that most of society possesses, which permits them a guaranteed license to issue an indictment of persecution of another's character. This is based solely from accusations and assumptions galvanized by the opinions of others to demolish their image or reputation. This is done before there is a close, careful examination of the information received to determine any true merit or misinterpretation. It's only meant to please the source from which it came.

Without proper guidance and research, the mind can develop a position simply out of the information it is being fed continuously through media outlets. This is because one has only allowed certain propaganda as a principal influence, thereby limiting oneself to certain forms of information. Therefore, it would be extremely difficult to present any other facts to those individuals whose decisions have been prematurely cultivated by committing to certain sources of information that they feel are most reliable. It causes them to fall into a state of denial, refusing to expand their minds as it relates to the rebuttal of the information that they chose to conceive. Ignorance is only the lack of knowledge that they choose to receive, not having the capacity to understand all knowledge that grants you the ability to decide based on truth and not personal preference.

So, before you consider condemnation or criticism of my first-degree murder charge, I propose the idea of research from different avenues so you can discover more substance rather than being comfortable with information that's just on the surface. The surface has no significance for the internal and always seeks to accommodate the external.

THINKING OUT LOUD

TURNEY COUNTY ANNEX
2017

Journal Entry

Whenever I grab a pen, I instantly begin to inscribe words between these lines, expressing myself in ways I've never deemed imaginable. Yet, in the midst of so much darkness and negativity as I fight this murder charge, God continues to provide His grace daily. He even blessed me with Will, who sits with me regularly to dissect scripture in the chapel or library.

God's grace turns a switch on the inside of me, which moves me to make tireless efforts to advance mentally and spiritually. I don't want to succumb to an environment that holds a majority of people whose mental capacity exceeds no further than the parking lot.

Experience can teach one something that neither books nor other humans can. That is why I praise and thank

God daily for allowing me to endure this journey despite laborious, violent oppression that endangers my safety. This experience has awakened me to identify all my characteristics that need to be rectified for me to become the man that God created me to be.

Emotionally, I managed through trials and tribulations. I even remained tranquil and persistent in the face of multiple circumstances that could've caused me to be despondent. Instead, I remained exuberant. Seeing how I'm turning away from my old self and toward the new one is amazing. Staying positive superseded the obstacle by staying resolute and industrious, allowing me to prevail. Only some can convey this process intentionally to those whom one encounters. I am hoping against hope to compel my spirit to the Utmost. I want to motivate and encourage myself despite my circumstances or challenges.

With open arms in closing, I permit you to sit in the theater of my mind to watch a movie of my thoughts. It will allow you to cultivate places where most deteriorate within them.

THANK YOU, SISTER

TURNEY CENTER
2017

Dear sister,

No selection of words can be used to describe your exuberant nature and compassionate heart coupling to a degree beyond measure. The tenaciousness you have displayed aligned with your relentless attitude despite any obstacle presented – somehow, you have continued to manage your emotional state by maintaining a level of serenity. And you did this without any manual or guide to withstand a confusing, discomforting, and complex struggle of someone else at the expense of your valuable time, resources, and energy. At your age, most could not fathom the thought of taking on such responsibility for the mistakes and mishaps of another, and that deserves more than applause to the utmost. It is indescribable beyond comprehension.

Regardless of the many false accusations of my character, you would not permit the bond of love to be neither broken nor swayed. You never allowed yourself to become ambivalent about who or what I became. You also never yielded to the opinions of the masses. You remained steadfast in supplying an incredible amount of unwavering support, love, and loyalty in a time of isolation and separation. This provided fuel to my engine. It gave inspiration and creativity to a man incarcerated in an institution full of despondency, which is the leading cause of the misdirection of the human existence. And that shall forever be engraved upon my heart.

In life, the people who love me for me despite the transgressions I have made still can have the clarity to see me for who they know I can become. For me, that is a confirmation of knowing who will be present for the problem *and* party. It confirms they will be celebratory of my blessings and never become disentangled in my burdens.

THE BATTLE

TURNEY CENTER
2017

Dear God,

    Complexity and confusion intertwined with frustration have matured into the depths of my soul. It came from the vital information in which I received. The groaning in my spirit has cultivated a grievance way beyond expression to man, leaving a task only for the Divine to heal. Upon reading the information about my son, an internal eruption had given way to a war brewing between my inner man and outer man. My son has tripped over the same situations that mirrored my past, and it pains me. In all sincerity and truth, my inner man maintained a level of tranquility while being moderate in the face of heavy opposition. On the other hand, my outer man was in total contradiction with the inner man due to his past transgression. My reflection of what it looks like through my eyes did not quite co-exist with my understanding to rectify the situation.

But my inner man, despite the many challenges, kept a channel to the divine. I was staying steadfast in the realm of the ultimate One. Rather than trying to be the only one obtaining revelation from the Divine, my outer man developed a sense of guilt amongst himself for the absence of the proper training a son needs as he develops from childhood to adolescence. My outer man continued to perpetuate a self-attack emotionally through a constant reminder of my inability to perform parenting obligations, which was caused by my incarceration. My times in jail resulted from my former conduct of selfish ways.

However, my inner man overwhelmed the outer man by being persistent in the knowledge of God through the Spirit, which continued to reveal to my soul that the tireless efforts I make to advance myself will reap its harvest in due time. While the wisdom I bestowed upon my children seemed to be abandoned during their times of temptation, they will avoid the pitfalls and mishaps I once endured. By every fiber that lies within my being, it's imperative that success is revealed to them, not concealed from them.

THE STORY OF CHAOS AND CONFUSION

ELECTRICAL CLASS, TURNEY CENTER

2017

To Kesha, my friend,

Usually, I would begin a passage by conveying everything in my heart. However, at this moment, I was halted by the desire to share a story about two individuals involved in a very intense and intimate relationship. The male's name is Chaos, and the female's name is Confusion.

First, it's important to understand the correlation between the two words so you can fully comprehend the magnitude of Chaos and how it coincides with Confusion. Chaos can be defined by very extreme confusion or disorder, and confusion can only occur through the lineage of chaos. For that reason, there is a dominance that chaos has if it is linked to simplicity. Eventually, confusion will arise due to its complexity.

Chaos did not display his emotional attachment to Confusion publicly, but privately, he harbored feelings invisible to the human eye. Selfishness and greed compelled Chaos to pamper the beast within him more than nurture the God living inside of him. In doing so, Chaos neglected the vital duty of providing assurance that consoles her need for security. Instead, he cultivated seeds of infidelity and disputes, awakening unexpected insecurity within Confusion.

Meanwhile, Confusion was only a recipient of who and what she was connected to. Initially, she possessed a genuine internal beauty that produced a light that externally ignited her exuberant nature. This alone distinguished her from her peers. Confusion became very unstable because of the lack of commitment she so desperately longed for that only existed in a world she did not live in. It became increasingly frustrating to seek after happiness only to receive the residue of agony and misery.

Not long after, Confusion was poisoned from laying in the bed of erogenous desires adjoining the corruption to whom she was connected. It created an immense component leading to barbarous acts of immaturity among them, polluted with verbal abuse. It kept the two in a puddle of turmoil contaminated with emotional roller coasters, resulting in domestic violence and ending in total separation.

In the midst of separation, Chaos wanders through a forest in a foreign land he is not accustomed to. Surviving in the forest, Chaos acquired a sense of direction with a new outlook on life. With the knowledge obtained, he developed the ability to provide healing without any selfish intent, leading him to witness fulfillment within Confusion. His awareness to adapt in the field of unfamiliarity humbled him in a way that lowered his ego while elevating his soul. And all of this allowed his spirit to lead, not his feelings, which created a world of peace that comforts instead of destroys.

At the same time, Confusion was no longer attached to Chaos which eliminates the mentality of chaos; therefore, she was awarded the opportunity to develop her identity by attending the university of self-evolution. Daily, she began to analyze and scrutinize herself under the statutes of God instead of the standards of the world. Prohibiting past behavior she once displayed, she has now emerged as an intelligent, career-driven, God-fearing woman who was not entangled in the web of loss and confusion; rather, she sat on the bench of contentment and compassion.

Chaos and Confusion reunite as new beings: Comfort and Compassion. They had hopes of rehabilitating an incomprehensible friendship once built upon a deceptive mentality compounded with an illusory train of thought.

Indescribable is the word that defines Compassion. Indescribable compassion is how she navigates the world without a global positioning system (GPS) in a traffic jam. She directs the lost not just by the words she speaks but by the actions she promotes.

Meanwhile, Comfort has gained spiritual wisdom from the Holy Spirit's guidance, imitating a high level of courage to initiate the passing of the bread that brings forth life. This contrasts with a man's desire to feed the internal hunger, only to remain in a state of starvation.

Together Comfort and Compassion have managed to surgically repair a damaged friendship. They are now walking in harmony and love exemplifying the growth accompanied by God's grace that was once unthinkable. No words can describe the image of sincerity and authenticity Compassion delivers towards Comfort as he strives endlessly among the woods of darkness, seeking to retrieve light from civilization. Despite the inequality between the two worlds in which they both reside, Comfort continues tirelessly, empowering Compassion by washing her spirit from the water of the word, which cleanses her soul – ultimately stimulating her mind.

Compassion is the epitome of loyalty. How willingly she immersed herself in uncertainty involving the forest Comfort. She walks in with selfless ambition, only the definition of her name being the sole purpose. At times, Comfort is taken aback by the compatible interest they both share. For so long, Chaos was masked by a lack of maturity, which hid the greatness buried deep within the depths of Confusion's pregnancy with the capacity to love beyond what was conceived from the womb of Compassion.

LETTER TO A FRIEND

TURNEY CENTER
2017

Dear Joslyn, my companion,

> "He who would accomplish little must sacrifice little; He who would achieve much must sacrifice much; He who would attain highly must sacrifice greatly."
>
> - James Allen -

Upon receiving your letter, I was astonished by the prominent display of beauty. It was so captivating from the pictures you sent. Words cannot describe the exuberance that quickly arose in almost nine years. Life is all about evolution. So, when an individual begins to proceed in age, the maturity level must reflect their age also. In this way, the state of one's thinking is congruent to the age one possesses instead of the size of the shoe one wears. The more knowledge one receives about any subject about self, health, finances, and God, the more their perspective changes due to the valuable information one obtained through discovery and research to become better.

It is the process of evolution. One must continue the growth and development of their mind through the word of God, allowing the Holy Spirit to remove them from the participation in the irrelevant activity as well as foolish disputes that are not conducive to the acceleration of one's progression. However, through consistent conversing among one another, it is pleasing to witness your level of determination and commitment, tirelessly thriving for the grand scale of financial attainment in hopes of ensuring a security blanket clothed with dreams, goals, and aspirations – all engraved in your daughter's spirit. She would be a recipient fulfilling the fruit reaped from the hard work birthed out of an inexpressible, inextricable, and godly mother. This is very attractive and well deserving of applause because of the overwhelming number of young, minority, single-parent women refusing to embrace the challenges accompanied by new opportunities that so eagerly call them to conceive greatness rather than seek shelter in the womb of mediocrity. Mediocrity only ever offers temporary comfort and cannot sustain their maturation into the fullness of God who created them to be. It is heart-wrenching.

Woman of God, it is very important that you personally take time out of time to grasp the essence compounded with the intimacy of God's word in its totality in efforts of acquiring His wisdom of discernment, permitting you to see that provision without purpose will not provide fulfillment. So, as you examine this glorious passage, let the words inscribed between these lines resonate deep within your spirit, touching your intellect and taking heed to the root of the message to gain a full, clear understanding of what is being said.

Oh, Heavenly Father, our Lord and Savior, Jesus Christ, I pray earnestly that you continue to protect and shower this beautiful, intelligent, funny, God-fearing woman with your abundance of love, humility, grace, and mercy while you propel her into her destiny filled with prosperity through the illustration of her poverty.

I'M NOT A PRODUCT OF WHERE I AM

1B POD, TURNEY CENTER
2017

Journal Entry

Ever since my incarceration, I have taken a strong approach to how I want to live the second half of my life compared to how I took for granted everything and everyone in the first half. After multiple vital mistakes throughout the process, I slowly began to come to myself by advancing my mind. This permitted me to think on a level exceedingly beyond the environment I was in. I now view this time of incarceration as spiritual school, not physical prison.

Suddenly I began noticing through conversing with the masses that I was now in a transition phase that subsequently separated me from the individuals I lived with. It was different because of the thought process I cultivated through my indefinite efforts to become a master of my environment. What I mean by the "separation" is that everyone from all ages to every ethnic group sounded the same. Their activity accompanied their behavior, which accompanied their mentality. And that did not agree with the mentality I had obtained from the knowledge and awareness I had acquired. Confusion replaced coalition because of each person's mindset, resisting mature discussions in exchange for personal directives. The discipline embedded in my spirit through daily practices helped me navigate how to avoid mediocre conversations that resulted in immature disputes, leading to unresolved conflicts and ending with a collision, all birthed from the mindset of the majority. This kept me mentally equipped to handle heavy opposition while still having the temperament to proceed with humility and compassion despite the indirect negative murmuring from my environment.

ENCOURAGEMENT TO A FEMALE FRIEND

TURNEY CENTER
2017

Dear Shanell, the beautiful,

Many moons have passed since our last correspondence. Still, I am forever grateful that you took time out to inquire about my well-being. I must admit that there is not a day that the sun sets without the thought of you crossing my mind. From inspecting your pictures, I was overwhelmed in awe by how sexy, beautiful and stunning you were from head to toe. Nevertheless, I am happy to write you to encourage you and impart knowledge as God imparts it to me.

My initial reaction to the letter I received from you was astounding. The enormous thoughtfulness compounded with the extensive preparation moved me the most. Your authenticity brought about an internal eruption that was indescribable.

Through thoroughly examining your thought process about the minor entanglement, you shared with me was very intriguing. I could identify with the growth in your character that resisted an immature response. You gave tireless efforts to rectify your thinking, which created mature outcomes.

Aided by godly humility, we must refrain from allowing how others treat us to dictate how we treat them by truly possessing Christ-like character despite the opposition. We must trust Him entirely, standing firm on His word, and not grow weary in well doing. (For in due season, we shall reap if we don't lose heart.)

We must bear His image to our young boys to produce faith, igniting the belief that will supersede any medical report in opposition to God's plan. I fully understand the continuous contemplation of providing a more promising future for your son, which will ultimately result from today's financial responsibility through the security that lies in the present. Allowing him all the possibilities to obtain his dreams is the epitome of a grown woman in pursuit of sacrificing for the greater good of her child. It deserves applause because most of today's society is unaware of how critical that way of thinking is.

Everyone (including myself) has events or moments in their history that shaped and molded them into who they are today. Therefore, when you explained the situation with your job while inquiring about the knowledge and experience gained from that particular time, it drew me closer to you. You allowed yourself to be vulnerable enough to invite me into the deeper essence of your being, trusting that I can be responsible and mature enough to keep classified information only for the benefit of us connecting on a more intimate level – to develop a friendship beyond anything we have imagined between us is truly at the core of my intentions.

Normally, I would hesitate to converse on subjects causing me to escape my comfort zone. However, the exchanges we have had in these prior months have awakened an irreconcilable emotion that has triggered a response due to the depth of our trials and tribulations that seem so identical to one another. I have not conversed with a woman of this magnitude – a woman whose supremacy solely rests upon the refusal to yield to the mediocrity of the masses. This shows me a lot of dedication and determination that I could sincerely see myself being a complementary piece of a puzzle put together by two incredible human beings.

As I continue this journey of evolution, I try to maintain balance within myself as to who I am, to who I have become. For example, many of my close friends have not changed how I have, so I stay cautious of my expectations of them. I don't want to be hypocritical because I was once there, and it was a struggle. Nevertheless, my friends often repeat the words "remember when" relating to our history. It is fine to visit the past if we acknowledge the growth and development over the years. But staying in the past is not connecting me to my destiny. I refuse to be bound to that place where I wasn't reaching for where I wanted to go. Separation equals success, so as difficult as it was, I had to cut the cord to those who only appeal to the worst parts of my past. If not, I would allow myself to sink into the seat of my company.

But God has bigger plans for me to succeed so that my kids and family can enjoy the fruits of my labor. There comes a point in a man's life – in my life – where, after countless encounters with death and excessive amounts of time incarcerated, that change is required in order to become the man God created me to be, being the son my mother always knew I could be, becoming the father my sons need me to be, and by His grace, the husband I was called to be. I have always possessed an exuberant spirit and a humorous personality that includes seriousness when necessary. I try to look at people, places, and things from a spiritual eye rather than a worldly view to resist negative emotions that will affect my reaction, altering my decisions based on how I perceive it in the natural, undermining how I should deny it in the spiritual.

Does that make sense? Ultimately, I strive to improve so my kids and other young men can model my behavior in all aspects of life, such as dealing with women, difficult situations, and overcoming. It is one of the objectives I plan to pursue with my boys through my non-profit organization called H.E.L.P. It will assist at-risk youth while empowering impoverished neighborhoods. It will rebuild and restore them through the transformation and the renewing of the mind one child at a time. So, with that said, a confirmation of the missive, whenever your time permits, would be tremendously appreciated very much.

ENCOURAGING A FRIEND IN CHRIST'S LOVE

TURNEY CENTER
2017

Dear Joslyn, my companion,

> "If you don't know you're lost, you can't be led And if you can't be honest, you can't be healed Before I could be rescued, I needed to realize I was stranded."
>
> – Lecrae -

As you carefully examine this glorious passage, I earnestly pray you allow the spirit of Christ that lives within us to enlighten your eyes to understanding. Unfortunately, time expired during our last conversation that did not allow me to elaborate on the goodness of God and how He is working in my life. I truly consider you someone special – a good friend that I can share the truth with. My sole purpose is to render a service to everyone I meet through the Word of God. I want to enrich, empower, and encourage everyone to become who God called them to be and to guide them away from the lust of the flesh.

Moving on God's behalf takes leaving the nest of comfort. As human beings, we never like to do or say anything that takes us out of that comfort state. However, with that mentality, we can get too complacent and miss out on our destiny. So, for that to happen, we must open ourselves to God so we can be moved by God. We will not always understand, but we still must trust and believe in the process.

I have been awarded wisdom that I don't deserve while being provided good men of God who have discipled me in an unexplainable way. Also, He has allowed my path to cross with a young lady. I believe He placed her here for me to bestow the glory He placed in me onto her to awaken her spiritual existence in whom she is in Christ rather than the world.

I tell you this because I trust you, and I love you, but I'm hoping to cultivate a friendship that is totally based on honesty - the same way we prayed together, allowing ourselves to be vulnerable in areas that were so unfamiliar.

I think our friendship can become stronger if we allow ourselves to look past who we once were together and look to who we have become. I invited you into my personal space to show you that I truly value our friendship, but I will never compromise the Word of God for my life. Still, I give you the opportunity to decide on how you want to proceed rather than keeping you in the dark.

Following Jesus does not just save us from a less fulfilling life or eternal separation from God. It also saves us to a life that can radically transform the world around us through the power of God. May God continue to bless you and your family. Whenever your time permits, a response to this glorious passage from my heart to yours would be tremendously appreciated.

A SPECIAL THANK YOU

AFTER ATTENDING BORN AGAIN CHAPEL
2017

Dear Auntie Bettie,

> "For I consider that the sufferings of this present time are not worthy to be compared with the glory which shall be revealed in us."
> Romans 8:18 (NKJV)

First and foremost, before I begin to invite you into my world, I want to thank my Lord and Savior Jesus Christ for His unwavering, undeniable love for me when I was solely driven by the lust and desires of this world.

The year was 2015 around November. I vividly remember going to a church service at Wayne County Annex. Entering the visitation gallery for this service has a different vibe than other services. The sisters and brothers of Born Again were very spirit-filled and very engaged with the assembly. They were conversing and shaking hands with everyone. I could sense the Holy Spirit moving in the atmosphere through revelation by sister Veronica, which I personally experienced.

Born Again allows two individuals to read scripture from the Old Testament and one from the New Testament. By the grace of God, this experience allowed me to become more courageous and bolder in speaking about my love for Jesus and His love for us through scripture. I have never spoken in a mass setting, nor was I given the opportunity. Born Again allowed one the opportunity for testimony as well, which was very rare from the services I had attended. As a result, I found myself waiting excitedly, thinking about every first Sunday. Plus, I was running to the podium to release God's word that I was studying that week.

I marveled at how these brothers and sisters were laying hands on inmates, casting out evil spirits, and healing. It was astonishing to witness the authority we have in person as opposed to watching it on T.V. Born Again allowed me to see the scripture fulfilled when Jesus said that you will do greater works than these. I am an ex-gang member who gave his entire life to Christ, and I am happier, more joyful, and more peaceful than I have ever been in my life. I encourage others to join Born Again for their tremendous work of saving brothers' lives through the word of God. I want to personally say that your ministry's light is shining behind these walls in Christ Jesus. Words can neither explain nor express the impact you all had on my life, but I am humbled and grateful for the time we spent together. I pray God's grace remains over the ministry. I love you guys.

LETTER TO MARIO

TURNEY CENTER
2018

Dear Mario,

> Therefore, I urge you, brothers and sisters, in view of God's mercy, to offer your bodies as a living sacrifice, holy and pleasing to God—this is your true and proper worship. Do not conform to the pattern of this world but be transformed by the renewing of your mind. Then you will be able to test and approve what God's will is—his good, pleasing and perfect will.
> Romans 12:1-2 (NIV)

I pray that this short missive brings forth some clarity regarding what matters most. I write to you not from a spirit of condemnation but of love. Our love extends beyond human comprehension, and I am praying diligently that Elohim will touch the depth of your soul in hopes of removing the veil of this world so you can experience the power of His word. Without physically touching our families or providing for them, people incarcerated perceive they are non-productive in their family's progression; however, people limit love to what they give as opposed to what they do.

In 1 John 3:18, the word of God reads: "My little children, let us not love in word or in tongue, but in deed and in truth." It is not about saying I love you but walking out that love through what we do daily. This shows how much we love our family.

I hear a lot and say very little, which leaves me to pray more. Bro, you got a lot going for yourself: family, kids, and a woman who loves you beyond the moon and back. Nevertheless, I love you, bro, and fervently pray to see you move beyond who you were to who you were created to be. Stay focused, big bro. Do not get distracted by your environment and lose sight of your purpose. I love you, big bro. I am praying for you!

WORDS OF ENCOURAGEMENT

TURNEY CENTER
2018

To Tasha, my sister,

As I paint this glorious canvas with divine cognizance, I urge you to take time out of your time to wisely inspect the message as opposed to the messenger. The nature of all humans who give their time, encouragement, money, or hand is to reciprocate that which is given. They may say with their mouth that nothing is wanted in return for their service; however, the noticeable response when gratitude is not shown displays the true intent within the heart that was there all along.

I understand that it can become increasingly frustrating and disappointing to not receive the level of affection or encouragement you bestowed on others. Searching for hands that seem to never get extended.

Constantly providing good deeds but somehow never to be remembered.

Personally, I want to encourage you to seek the approval of God instead of the approval of man. It's never what people say about you that counts, but what *you* say about yourself can stop you from reaching your destiny.

The Bible says that you are fearfully and wonderfully made. God loves you and wants to use you to extend His kingdom while being His example of love. Never let what people do to you or what they don't do for you contaminate the uniqueness residing within you. Be not weary in well doing. For in due time, you shall reap if you don't lose heart.

Before I end this letter, I want to be clear that I am a servant of Jesus Christ who came to inform, inspire and impart divine revelation that can transform and guard your heart. For out of the heart flows the issues of life. Please do not thank me. Thank my Lord and Savior, Jesus Christ. I hope my words have encouraged you.

THE CLEAR-UP

TURNEY CENTER
2018

Dear Shanell, the beautiful,

Our communication became like a pair of intertwined shoelaces, which created a misunderstanding due to the 14-year absence between us. I am forever grateful and appreciative of you, though, for taking time out of your schedule to send me a card filled with such warmth and meaning. Plus, the pictures mirror the pure essence of God's beautiful creation.

Please understand that every action committed was done not out of ill intent but to properly combat the situation at hand. For instance, the removal of your name, along with my aunts, was conducted in a manner I felt was conducive to preventing any life-threatening ramifications stemming from the audacious actions of another.

Amid that semi-separation, I received a compelling revelation of who I was and how that propelled me into who I've become. All this was done by an indescribable touch from the Creator Himself. Spiritually, I have been awakened in a way that is truly beyond human logic. But the fiery trial that has simultaneously come against me with my current murder charge (and everything surrounding that) has allowed me to surrender the perfected purpose of why I was created rather than the self-righteous stubbornness I previously demonstrated. Humbly, I must admit the mistakes made on my behalf along the way that could have prevented the distance between you and me. A conscious decision was made to focus solely on God and my well-being. In hopes of spiritual fulfillment, I neglected friendships without carefully considering the psychological effect it had on you and others. For example, I also disconnected from gang life and other people from my past.

Forsake not the thought of you never existing during this laborious but fulfilling period. Do not negate the power of prayer expressed sincerely and genuinely on your behalf despite your nonexistence in my life.

Before I end this glorious missive, I was captivated by your willingness to deliberately decisively choose a card that was more symbolic in meaning. Upon my departure, I pray and hope the words inscribed in this letter resonate deep within the crevice of your spirit to alleviate your soul from the mental complexity involving this incomprehensible situation.

LETTER TO MY BROTHER

TURNEY CENTER
2018

Dear Roshawn,

> "that he no longer should live the
> rest of his time in the flesh for the lust
> of men, but for the will of God."
> 1 Peter 4:2 (NKJV)

Long before receiving your missive, I was grieved by your decision that jeopardized your freedom. Nevertheless, the feeling of astonishment was evident upon grasping your glorious paradox. Before I proceed, I need you to carefully examine the depth of the words you are about to read, so you can wholeheartedly understand the process of metamorphosis in Christ Jesus.

I have forsaken the comfort of the creation to abide in the holiness of the Creator. I have abandoned the playground of Loki Baby, humbly returning to the residence of Quinton Mostella. I have disconnected from the deception of man's doctrine, now heeding only God's voice and truth. The water I used to drink of this world kept me in a state of greed as opposed to the water of God's word that kept me in a place of contentment. For I speak not of myself, but it is Him that lives in me and speaks to you. A wise man once told me, "Whenever you discover who you are, you'll discover you don't fit."

Honestly, this trial that has come against me is all part of God's plan of shaping and molding me in the process of preparation for what has not yet been revealed. Understand, my beloved brother, that the things which have happened to me have actually turned out for the purpose of spreading the gospel, so that it has become evident to the city, and to all the rest, that my chains are in Christ (Philippians 1: 12-13). No need to worry. Everything is on schedule according to His divine appointment. Yet, while His manifestation remains avail, confessing, trusting, and believing in His word is my primary focus despite the outcome.

It is crucial in these perilous times that, as men, we become aware of who we are and whose we are. If not, the perpetual state of spiritual poverty will spill over into generations to come. I vividly remember saying, *I am a man before I am anything*, but the question should be raised: Are we anything before becoming a man? In life, we are given three names: The one given at birth, the one we are called by others, and the one we acquire in life on earth. What name do you go by?

Upon my departure, I am forever grateful that you took time out of time to inquire about my well-being as well as enlighten me on the blessings and burdens that currently exist in your life. I pray earnestly that you would permit Christ Jesus to not only save you but be Lord over you. As we continue to strive fervently through these shallow waters, keep your eyes as those of a fish, for they never blink or close. I leave you with a love that no love can explain.

I have stopped pursuing the possessions of the earth while freely receiving the gifts of heaven. I have drowned my ego and pride; they lay waste in the pond of destruction. The womb of the spirit brings gentleness and humility out of the river of resurrection.

ENCOURAGING MY FRIEND'S SISTER

TURNEY CENTER
2018

Dear brother,

Pardon my delay, my little brother; however, despite my hectic schedule, it was a must I set aside time out of time to reply back to your glorious missive. Astonished is a word that could be used to describe the feeling of the revealing of your name on the envelope. I am exuberant to see you compensating yourself through this laborious situation. Stay focused and steadfast and advance yourself mentally, physically, and spiritually because the victory is to complete the assignment, not change the critic's mind.

As I carefully examined your letter, I was taken aback your statement about your sister. For years now, I diligently tried to place some knowledge upon her, but I understand that some individuals perform and think on a level they see throughout their lives. They do this instead of who they were born to be. So, for her to even attempt to rectify her situation or mental state, she must be able to identify the root cause of her thoughts and actions. This occurs through self-examination, but it would be highly unlikely due to all the irrelevant entertainment she is consumed with daily.

I want to give you this analogy between the mind and a car so you can fully understand the depth of what I am talking about. It is true without gas: Without it, a car cannot move despite how good it looks or how much it costs. Without gas, it cannot do what it's designed to do. The same is true for your mind if you only inject messages or images of your surroundings – would we expect you to advance beyond your environment? If you wish to get the maximum performance out of a car, then you will have to put the appropriate gas in it so it can fulfill its duty.

So, you must understand that one's actions are equivalent to the intake of information being withheld in their brain. To travel for an extensive number of miles, you must fuel the car to its capacity to reach the desired destination. Therefore, my questions would be: *Does your sister have enough stored in her mental capacity to exceed life's temptations and struggles, or does she only possess enough to cease her true potential?* Whether or not she will humble herself to receive instruction to push past what she sees is yet to be determined. In order to overcome poverty (financial, spiritual, and emotional), she needs only to raise her level of vision. The lack of any type is found within a change of thinking.

Ever since I unattached myself from the cage through the embracing of God's garment of love, my life has never been more meaningful. By God's grace, I have reached the pinnacle of who I was created to be as opposed to who I was portraying. It is time to serve the Creator instead of the creation to fulfill my purpose to revive, restore, and rebuild my community I once destroyed through the irresponsible and illegal activity that kept my people in bondage. This fiery trial that has come up against me will be over soon, and I will be down there until then. Just know the love I have for you is not of this world but of Him (Jesus), who overcame the world.

APPRECIATION FOR MY BROTHER'S LOVE

TURNEY CENTER
2018

Dear bro,

> "The happiness of your life depends upon the quality of your thoughts."
> - Marcus Arelius -

Over the course of these past few years, Quinton has closely observed the maturation process through consistent conversation between you and him. Quinton is astounded by your ability to remain focused and steadfast on your future amid opposition arising in your present.

You have displayed a high level of humility to refrain from responding to conflict in accordance with the mentality of the environment you were developed in.

Nevertheless, that way you have managed to navigate through shallow waters with reason and patience, fully understanding the livelihood of those who could be impacted severely by your decisions, is a true testament to the self-awareness Quinton so lacked at your age.

Quinton marvels at how you resist the applause from the fans but seek wise counsel from the coach of instruction. In this day and age, it is very uncommon to witness young men with your prestige who are sincerely open to receiving refinement through righteous correction by the word of God. Soon thereafter, the soul becomes cleansed from the filth of this perverse world, producing a polished spirit in hopes of edifying the mind to concentrate on perfecting one's purpose instead of one's person.

Always stay mindful of how precious freedom is and fragile life can be. Never forsake the simplicity of the lesser in your pursuit of the greater. Because millions have inadvertently mishandled the luxury of the simple. They are drunk off the benefits of the extravagant, and now their minds are incarcerated with extreme exotic imagination. It is due to the inability to grasp the reality of attainment through civilization, which hangs in the closet of uncertainty. Negate not the promise that sleeps in the bed of patience, for the satisfaction of your peers mirrors where you have been but are clueless to where you are going.

A LETTER TO MY SONS: QUINTAVEOUS AND QUINZARIUS

TURNEY CENTER

2018

Dear sons of mine,

Understand that our situations as young boys mirror one another. Carefully examine that the absence of your father in your life is identical to the absence of my father in my life as a young boy. During my teenage years, I desperately yearned for the attention and affection of the co-conspirator in God's plan of putting me here on earth. Somehow, I disguised the loneliness through the fulfillment of sports and male attachment that resembled the preconceived notion I thought a man should be. Yet and still, as I matured silently, my soul was crying internally, never to express the agony externally and hurt I was suffering from.

At times I felt a sense of abandonment, resulting in me gravitating to a gang that initially felt like a sense of acceptance I had been deprived of all my life. Without the proper self-awareness or seeing the real value of a woman, I disrespected myself and countless women through the misinterpretation of sex. I was mimicking the actions of other men I admired instead of seeing those things I so lacked. Shortly thereafter, I masked my emotions with reckless smoking combined with the over-consumption of alcohol, which impaired my vision and hindered my mental capacity to think beyond my environment. It caused me to depend solely upon my environment through illegal activity.

Humbly, I ask that you let me be your GPS in assisting your navigation through adolescence. Allow me to impart my knowledge that will benefit you tremendously. I can only be of service to you through your willingness to participate in expressing your concerns, fears, doubts, and struggles you will face. I truly apologize for my immature and selfish decisions that caused the separation between us in these perilous times. Always remember to never make snap decisions in temporary moments that have lifelong consequences.

Before I depart, I must mention how much I love you all. I am proud of you both, and it's only when I became aware of who I am in Christ Jesus that I could identify all the behaviors of my past that led to the present, but it will not determine my future.

APPRECIATION OF YOUR GENEROSITY

TURNEY CENTER
2018

Dear Bobby,

In conversing with my little brother yesterday, he informed me about your sincere thoughtfulness and efforts to try and reconcile the difficulties that are at the forefront of my life. No words can explain the insurmountable gratefulness and appreciation that I am filled with concerning your concern for my obstacles. Thank you for giving my brother some money for me.

One must understand that the actions of a man are in total agreement with this thinking. So whatever one does is in response to how one is thinking. I say that to say your actions are an exemplification of your thoughts, which have blossomed into the action you have taken, accompanied by the attributes of loyalty, compassion, graciousness, patience, and longsuffering. These things combined with an authenticity beyond human comprehension, which lay beneath the souls of individuals today due to the inability to remain committed to one's burden as opposed to his blessing.

The transformation I encountered in my thinking resulted from my incarceration. Still, the grace of God has given me the ability to detach my spirit from alignment with an infected soul through a body possessed by demonic forces that allowed villainous actions to surface. Those actions portrayed who I was instead of who I had become by being intoxicated by earthly possessions, which are only temporary. This led me to a life saturated with headaches, heartaches, and hardships. Meanwhile, unknowingly having the full capacity to identify the divine mindset that was imparted within me from the day I was born. I was clinging to heavenly possessions causing me to experience peace, joy, comfort, abundance, and understanding that will ultimately divert you from experiencing the pitfalls that stand in my face at this present moment.

As you examine this glorious missive, carefully pay attention so you can understand the complexity of what is being spoken. I want you to fully grasp the poverty of the situation stemming from the power that lies within the choices I made. This was always in contrast to the prosperity I could obtain from the promise I could receive through our Lord Jesus Christ. I don't want you to make the same mistakes. Before I exit this letter, always remember that you must never envision your crosses as destinations. For they are only interruptions to your celebrations.

A CLEAR LETTER

ANNEX
2018

Dear Clear,

> "So as to live for the rest of the time in the flesh no longer for human passions but for the will of God."
> 1 Peter 4:2 (ESV)

Although a lot of time has passed since our last conversation, the thought of reaching out to you has become increasingly overwhelming. Before I elaborate on the events that have transpired, I want to first and foremost thank our Lord and Savior, Jesus Christ for the divine connection between us. I remember how we used to work together, work out together, and watch T.D. Jakes together. You were truly a God send to me, and I've always appreciated your wisdom. Therefore, I'm writing this letter to share how my life has changed for the good.

Ever since I departed from the annex, God has had His mighty hand working in my life. After close examination and revelation from the Holy Spirit, I thank God for all my adversaries who played a pivotal role in the changes I face today. Without this heavy opposition, I would have never encountered the next dimension of life that I am in currently.

God has delivered me from the alignment of the gang, Gangster Disciples (GD) and has set me totally free on September 8, 2017. I have never been so free and alive since I was a kid. The more I kept reading and digesting God's word and fellowship with brothers like yourself, God was changing my heart into who He created me to be as opposed to who I believed I needed to be for other people.

Personally, I want to thank you for the awareness you bestowed upon me during our brief time spent together. You cannot fathom the impact you have had on my life. I am at a loss for words to find that can describe or explain God's goodness and mercy, for which I am not worthy but thank God for. Personally, I was writing to enlighten you on the progression relating to my walk with Jesus and tell you I love you. I am praying for you, and I hope you and your family have a beautiful and blessed Thanksgiving.

I APOLOGIZE FOR ME

TURNEY CENTER
2018

Dear Latoya,

Personally, I want to take this time to rectify my immaturity and wrongdoings. While I have told you before, I want to reiterate to you that what I said and did doesn't define who I am. As I reflect on the harsh reality we had at times, I can vividly remember the physical, mental, and emotional abuse that I distributed. My heart breaks knowing that I treated you that way when all you were looking for was the equivalency of the love you were giving. I was selfish and irresponsible because I couldn't stand on my word for trying to imitate the world.

I was treating my body similarly to yours. Because I was mistreating my temple with alcohol, drugs, illicit sex, and a poisonous tongue that led to foul language, heartache, and disappointment in our relationship. Until a person understands who they are in Christ and what Christ has done for them, it's impossible to treat a person like they would want to be treated without selfish intent. It was always about "me" instead of "we" because of my condition. A relationship without reciprocity will never last. Anytime you give more than you intend to get, then you will stay in a state of disappointment. Understand Loki only wanted what he could get from you. In contrast, Quinton wants to give you everything Jesus has given him.

ENCOURAGEMENT FOR MY NIECE

TURNEY CENTER
2018

Dear beloved niece,

I open this missive hoping against hope these words produce a mature level of understanding between you and your father. I spoke with him and heard his grief regarding his inability to articulate his perspective on how to love you from a distance.

Please understand the relationship between your mother and father, be it good or bad, by no means diminishes the unconditional love he consistently expresses to me about his firstborn. As we grow older, we tend to take the little things for granted. As you rise every morning in the process of beautifying yourself for school, does it ever dawn on you that this was a learned behavior by someone who loves you? Personally, I witnessed the joy and passion your father displayed in preparing you for class every morning. Your laughter and his smile way back then allow me to recognize the love a father has for his child.

People underestimate the things they have in their lives for the things they desire to have. How many of your friends' fathers are in prison, on drugs, or are simply not present for the meaningful day-to-day activities in the lives of their children? Have you ever taken the time to ask your father why the departure from Columbia to Virginia was so urgent? Imagine if he stayed in Columbia: Would the letter you are now reading be from your uncle or an incarcerated father due to our lifestyle? Honestly, would you prefer your father write you from prison or visit you from Virginia for every special moment that arises in your life?

On the scale, love can never be imbalanced unless it is entertained by selfishness. You will always be your daddy's girl, even today as a young woman. Not long, a time will manifest when the nurturing love he provided for you will mirror the sacrifices you will make for your family to assist your daddy's needs as his age increases. Money can be restored. Health can be restored. But time cannot. Never let the precious moments and opportunities to bridge the gap pass you by.

HOW WE STARTED

BUILDING TRADE
2018

Dear Kesha, my friend,

>I write this to describe our relationship and how it began through basketball.

1st Quarter

>"Our story may not be a happy beginning but that doesn't make us who we are.
>It's the rest of our story that defines who we chose to become."
>- Kung Fu Panda -

Infatuated by her exterior essence, the seed was planted in his subconscious that impelled the initial conversation. A fire was sparked in the category of compatibility once her undaunted competitiveness was displayed in the game of basketball, a sport that he so loved himself. Simultaneously, basketball practice became a little more intriguing because of his curiosity about the physical qualities that she possessed. Fascinated by how scrumptious she appeared in basketball shorts, he was eager to discover the personality residing within the container as opposed to lusting after the physical intimacy.

Despite the distance in the numbers that indicated their maturity, his exuberance expired in the imagination of sex rather than first journeying through the realm of dating. His inability to withdraw from sexual uprising caused a spirit of persuasion to take root. Ultimately, he felt manipulation was needed to accomplish this pleasure, derived from a severe craving from an animalistic nature he never knew he had.

Shortly thereafter, the images that were once implanted in his subconscious had become engraved into the depths of her subconscious. Consequently, the mating of two unequally yoked teenagers whose perception of intimacy was in total disagreement with one another led to the perpetuation of intense passion without the garment of provision.

2nd Quarter

> "The ultimate measure of a man is not where he stands in moments of comfort and convenience, but where he stands at times of challenge and controversy"
> - Dr. MLK Jr. -

After consistent irresponsible sexual activity, her womb had become a nest holding the promise of a precious fetus. Amid this glorious process, their relationship became very debilitated because of his fear of what was yet to come. Being ill-equipped coincided with a lack of awareness, and it didn't alleviate the mounting expectations and pressures to perform on a level that he had never witnessed before. Tormented by the doubts and worries, it enabled him to communicate his concerns to her appropriately. But that caused him to flee, neglecting his sole duty of providing stability, love, and peace in a pivotal time when she very much deserved a sense of security.

Meanwhile, we rested in a deadlock of unresolved issues, constantly igniting fiery confrontations, dysfunctional discussions, and synchronized with passionate bedtime harmony. It created a collection of confusion tightly wrapped in a night of passion, only to be awakened in the puddle of anxiety stemming from the silent cries buried deep within the soul. The precious fetus that lay so peacefully in the water of uncertainty now has been called to the wilderness of conflict. Within the fertile soil of the womb of darkness, the seed was birthed into the existence of light, and it totally changed their lives.

3rd Quarter

> "God doesn't give you the people you want,
> he gives you the people you need. To help
> you, to hurt you, to leave you, to love you and
> make you the person you were meant to be."
> - Anonymous -

Not long after receiving one of the greatest gifts from God, he became disobedient to the plan of God, which led to a complete separation from God, ending in a place where he would totally rely upon the favor of God. Disconnected from civilization, he fell into a fixation with transformation. It was effectively accomplished by countless hours of reading and self-examination of who he was as opposed to who he wanted to become. During this harrowing and zealous journey, he discovered the power of Him who lived in him was greater than the power of the people and the things around him. That would ultimately change the people connected to him. Separation from them gave him the chance to evaluate. He surpassed his former life and friends through humility, which gave way for him to receive instruction from God. The more studying and writing he did, he increased his enlightenment, producing glorious fruit intertwined with divine revelation.

Therefore, her ear to hear has now become vital in processing information in alignment with what has been exposed to her, contrary to what she has been accustomed to. Meanwhile, her vision has become sensitive to the presentation in relation to the majority of other people's opinions. It was due to her ability to identify the intellectual, Godly characteristics in the minority that are so often overlooked.

Suddenly the veil has been removed from the hearts of the individuals to establish communication of truth, propelling a loyal friendship beyond human logic.

4th Quarter

> "Love is patient and kind; love does not envy or boast; it is not arrogant or rude. It does not insist on its own way; it is not irritable or resentful; it does not rejoice at wrongdoing, but rejoices with the truth. Love bears all things, believes all things, hopes all things, endures all things." Love never ends!
> 1 Corinthians 13:4-8 (ESV)

The progression to deprive yourself of yourself indicates your purpose, which lies in your capacity to serve beyond the fulfillment of yourself. Consider calculating the width and length before investing time and energy, preventing significant mishaps due to the lack of logic and reasoning. Carefully evaluate your environmental stability as a crucial component to seeing your future rather than becoming complacent with your present. Never neglect the daily inspection of your diagram of those who only care for you in your crisis but are unable to carry you to your deliverance. Stay sober and diligent of those same individuals who are always present for the party but absent from the problem, eagerly anticipating the blessing while scampering from the burden.

Detect the essence of your soul through endless navigation of the Word that cleanses the filth from your temple. Constantly renew your mind through spiritual digestion, equipping yourself with the proper awareness to not devalue your physical. Continue your enthusiasm for increasing your education and independence, which will register more fully with the ones you carry in the water as opposed to those you stand in the dirt. Remember, the vision is for an appointed time. Forsake not what you lost but multiply what you have left. The manifestation of what is to come has not yet been revealed. So, hold firmly to the pain and struggle of today. You will then be able to rejoice and cherish the promise of tomorrow.

THE RESURRECTION OF A MAN

TURNEY CENTER
2018

Journal Entry

He was awakened with cold sweats as if standing in the rain. Astonished by the vision captured during this journey away from existence. Resting within the depths of his dream and reality, his mind is compiled with anxiety. Quarterly, the harsh reminder of Lenny's destination was imprinted by two numbers upon a sheet of paper. Filled with uncontrolled anger that even an infant can detect, hate was spewing from his lips.

Trying his best to cope and maintain, needles in and out of Lenny's arm was the only way to ease the pain. His veins were toxic, equivalent to the deterioration of his liver due to rotten metal that produced homemade liquor. Blinded by complaining, running down the path of aggravation, compounded by procrastination. More often than not, he finds himself lost in aimless deliberation.

His reputation limits change because he fears humanity's perspective. Lenny's identity revolves around vain possessions, empty quarrels, and misguided desires hindering the completion of his purpose. Loyalty is vital for camaraderie. "We all we got" was the motto for surviving poverty. A part of him has always been tied to others because he was permanently scarred by abandonment from his father and mother. Stains of betrayal poisoned his ability to converse. Fifty-one years got him feeling *What is life worth?*

He loves to feed himself the scraps of the world. Meanwhile, his spirit is silently crying out for the nourishment of the Word. He decided to go to a few church services, but nothing changed. Then, one night, Lenny cried out to God after reading Matthew 11:28 and his life was never the same. His heart began to reflect the poetry of the scriptures. He no longer serves the fear of death but cannot wait to depart. Finally, he was set free by the blood, which provided him a new heart.

Cleansed from worry, the mess he made became his story. Jesus changed his life. He now rejoices, giving him all the praise, honor, and glory.

ENCOURAGEMENT FOR YOUR TIME OF NEED

TURNEY CENTER
2018

Dear Latoya,

> "Whenever there is the emergence of the new,
> we can confront the recalcitrance of the old."
> - Dr. Martin Luther King, Jr. -

Many moons have passed since the last time I have taken time out of time to address you in this particular manner – a manner that is not of a romantic relationship but of encouragement. After conversing with you, I felt a sense of urgency to alleviate a soul silently crying out *Help me!* That contrasted with the lips that masked the hurt. Understand that for you to receive instruction, you must be open; however, for you to be open, you must be humble.

It is not always about what you see but more so how you interpret what you see. The gateway to receiving instruction from me lies solely in your perception of how you view me. The manifestation of the light from the words I speak can only be manifested through the decisions you make. In regard to your perspective as *Loki telling me what to do,* or *Could this be God informing me through His Spirit, which resides in Quinton*? In order to rectify a situation, one must provide the courage to identify the root of the situation. Change can only prevail through the tunnel of pure honesty in hopes of liberating a mindset attached to an inherent behavior chained in a body of bondage. This can only occur by a transformation in your thinking accompanied by a cleansing of your soul, which brings forth spiritual resurrection. Only when you start digesting spiritual food can you negate carnal thinking and alter carnal behavior.

Have you taken the initiative to examine the consistent tongues that tell you empty promises left with no solutions? Does it seem obvious that you perpetually align yourself with this exact type disguised in an orthodox vessel, possessing qualities congruent to the prior, hoping to receive a different outcome that is beyond comprehensible? Have you neglected the Giver that lives within you for the gift from man which sustains you but cannot fulfill you? Everything and anything you seek and admire in them, you can find in Him. Have the demands of your decisions distracted you from your purpose, becoming unaware of diligently pursuing the perfection of your person?

I pray that this glorious missive opens the eyes of your understanding to solely depend on God, who breathes the breath of life in you. Do not be tempted by Satan, who manipulates you by the feelings that penetrate inside you.

THE DEPTH OF MY ENVIRONMENT

THE POD
2018

Journal Entry

Finally, the shackles have been cut from the ankles of my past. The deeply lacerated wounds from the stumble are the anchor to my humility. I am enjoying the exuberance of the present amid uncertainty awaiting in my future. Complaints and complacency are the traits of comrades who reside in conformity because of the limitations of their thinking. Isolation, in conjunction with individualism, is rare and strange to the masses who breathe air from the lungs of fear attached to the body of companionship. Authority with misguided power mishandles its obligation of equality by exercising the symptoms of inequality.

I was internally in bondage from the perception of superiority while externally examining the inferiority. It was cultivating an aroma of enragement that could cause tragic hostility. Idealism is hidden deep within the depths of the irresponsible person who refuses to see the blessing, especially if he's solely focusing on the burden. Envy and jealousy are tainted spirits entangled with a material mindset masked by a high level of insecurity.

Loneliness is displayed by extreme playfulness, according to those who desperately long for the touch of a woman but often retreat to the rapture of man. Education is buried in the graveyard of excitement from the games that provide quick fulfillment, but they perpetuate lifelong incompetence about who one is and where one is going.

Articulation and manipulation are wonder twins of the cunning who seek to exploit the meek through carnal eyes from the assumption of them being weak. On the other hand, passion and persistence resemble the faces of the vigorous who consistently seek to devour the improper infractions placed upon them by a rigged system.

It's vitally important to never underestimate the potential of those you are around solely based on the position they are in, contradicting who they are in alignment to where they are going.

MY REALITY

THE LIBRARY
2018

Journal Entry

"I knew right there in prison that reading had changed forever the course of my life. As I see it today, the ability to read awoke inside me some long dormant craving to be mentally alive. . . . My home made education gave me, with every additional book I read, a little more sensitivity to deafness, dumbness, and blindness that was affecting the black race in America."
- Malcolm X -

After a substantial amount of time incarcerated, I have developed a level of patience beyond the science of human logic. Daily, I inspect the mentality of my surroundings through careful observation according to the gestures people display with the words they speak. My ears have become a key tool for advancement and discernment by solitary engagement instead of full participation. My right ear permits me to advance by understanding that the mentality of a person whose identity and self-worth revolve around their condition instead of their position. My left ear allows me to cross-examine the spirit for which one comes by the actions centered around who one serves in relation to who one rejects.

My hands have become godly weapons of divine impartation of knowledge upon the masses who are blinded by my dream while dead to my reality. My eyes are constructed as windows, peaking at a future dressed in the garment of limitless opportunities and camouflaged with a robe of restoration to a misguided generation. My legs symbolize more than aerobics but are integral components of running my purpose rather than standing in the mud of my past. My arms resemble undeniable love that stretches beyond the restrictions of this world while reflecting the image of Jesus, who overcame this world. My body is an instrument that plays a very distinctive tone but is willing to invite the sounds of other instruments to create a perfect harmony coinciding with a beautiful song.

My mind is so congested with so much scripture that it is overflowing with unexplainable truth, causing me to suffer from a serious case of constipation by divine revelation. I never knew I could prosper beyond the expectations of my peers until I escaped the grasp of my fears, manifesting itself within the last nine years.

SOMETIMES, I WISH I WAS DEAF

POD
2018

Journal Entry

Sometimes I imagine what life would be like if I was deaf, having the ability to pursue every thought without interruptions, to be in hot pursuit of attainment that nullifies daily empty rhetoric. If man speaks over 2500 words a day with 146 people, how many words does he speak that enlighten, encourage, or uplift not just him but others? Nonsensical words that have no merit seem to implant themselves in the soul of humanity, producing aimless endeavors.

What if I could not hear humanity physically but could only hear one spiritually? The only word that penetrates the depth of being is the Word that created the essence of my being. The only watering that could nourish my soul and prevent desolation is the word of God, which causes illumination and escapes the wrath of incarceration.

Swimming in the ocean of vanity, I refuse to let the wave of mediocrity take me under; therefore, I resist the plunder from the tempest. Yet, waves seem to increase, and the struggle becomes unbearable, clinging to the rock that is invisible.

RUNNING

NEAR THE BARBED WIRE FENCE
2018

Journal Entry

The Promised land requires you to forsake your comfort to attain your destiny.
- T.D. Jakes -

As I continue to strive in this perpetual struggle despite the opposition and indifference I face, I seek the promise from the Hand of provision. However, my undeniable faith in Christ gives me the courage to face the uncertainties of the future. It will give my tired feet new strength as I continue forward toward the city of freedom. I must admit that there are days when my mind becomes weary from the travel that seems to never end.

Daily discipline and studying the word of God help me navigate the world of the lost. Not having the word of

God is like a blind man traveling a dark road, trying to find his way back home but finding himself somewhere else. My current situation raised a man from a boy. I was blinded by the apparel of the world. Now, in contrast, a man in love with gifts of the Spirit. I never knew this life existed until I left the prince's apartment to live in the mansion with the king. I am often astonished after permitting the Spirit of God access to my soul, transforming me into a new being.

Gazing out my window, I see the semblance of freedom through the barbed wire entangled by the broken justice system, sitting on the shoulders of Jim Crow rather than the constitution and moral principles America so prides herself on. Now that I am passionately running toward my purpose, I still smell the smoke from my past. Nevertheless, the smoke is a reminder of what I used to do and used to be. I was opposed to the light, which now illuminates who I am. I am now maximizing my potential for who I was created to be.

ENCOURAGEMENT FOR MY BROTHER

TURNEY CENTER

2019

Dear brother,

Before I write my thoughts upon this glorious passage, O Father, I pray in the name of the Holy One, blessed be He, creator of Heaven and Earth. May the words You give me ignite the fire that has laid dormant within my brother's soul. I have hopes of him one day pursuing the relationship you so long for with his whole heart rather than mere lip service in the name of Yahweh, El Elyon, God Most High. Amen.

I received your missive last night. Words can't explain the exuberance of seeing my family. Through the pictures, I see the power of God moving through my family. The Bible says that children are the heritage of the Lord, and my little niece and nephew are beautiful.

Despite where you are spiritually, I want to salute you for the father, son, uncle, and friend you are. You are doing an incredible job with yourself - managing your business affairs while always being a blessing to me. I thank my Lord Jesus Christ for a brother who loves not with words but more so with action. I want to tell you to never cease to grow and love, not just family and friends but also those who despise and use us. Like Stephen in Acts 7:60 said, "Lord, do not charge them with this sin."

As I examined your letter, I was inspired by how you expressed the significance of what I say at times. I want you to know that it's the Spirit working through me. Through obedience, I have emptied myself to be used by him. That is why my words may sometimes speak to your soul - a holy vessel operating in the capacity of a holy God, under the divine authority of the Holy Spirit, awakening that which only sleeps within you.

I never knew this life existed. Literally, the Holy One, blessed be, He teaches me His word because I so long for His presence like I once did with women. Understand that He provides His peace that surpasses all understanding through Christ Jesus. In other words, when one asks, *How can you not be mad or disturbed by what happens to you?* It's because I see what happened to Jesus.

Plus, I see His purpose and plan in it. Everyone needs a Judas to push them into the purpose God has for them. God used multiple individuals to perfect His divine plan for my life (Romans 8:28).

I say all of this to speak of your situation with your family. Bro, he got a stronghold that he is fighting. I know it gets frustrating and disturbing, but this situation pushes you into your destiny and a new level of spiritual maturity with Jesus Christ. You've got to stand in the gap: Don't stop praying for them because despite them believing in Christ, them folks are unlearned. They are not walking in the spirit. I don't want you to get this life confused by what they say they don't know. This is just tradition to them.

My Lord has shown me how to fight with the Word of God when situations look gloomy; yet, when Christians are contrary to the Word, it's because they don't perceive it correctly. The Bible tells me my strength comes from the Lord, so I'm all in, just like I was with the world, GD, basketball, etc. I am all in. I try, through the Holy Spirit's guidance, to do everything the Word tells me. Then I will be transformed and cleansed by the Word while manifesting *into* the Word. As a result, when people see or hear me, it will reflect that which is Christ Jesus.

Isaiah 40:31 says, "But those who wait on the Lord Shall renew their strength; they shall mount up with wings like eagles, They shall run and not be weary, They shall walk and not faint." Without Jesus, I would have gone left, but His grace, mercy, and love kept me unmovable and unwavering despite that which came against me. He who is in me is greater than he who is against me. It is a process by its time, Big Bro. We got to raise the next generation on the Word of God and not the world. It is pivotal in these perilous times that we show them Christ as opposed to man. I miss you, and I love you. Tell my sister-in-law I am always praying for you both, including your marriage and family. The day will come when these words will be manifested into actions mirroring us both doing the will of God.

Oh, Father, continue showing my brother your power and wisdom. Oh, Father, I pray you guide, protect, and keep them all in your ways. Let them trust totally in you, leaning not on their own understanding but acknowledging you in all their ways and you will direct their paths. In Jesus' name, Amen. (Proverbs 3:45)

WHO YOU ARE IN CHRIST

TURNEY CENTER
2019

Dear Shanell, the beautiful,

Throughout my existence, I searched tirelessly for the love I so desperately longed for that could only come from Jesus. Unaware of the ramifications from my decisions, I became spiritually ill, laying in contamination, appeasing the outer man while death occurred to the inner man.

Without being spiritually inclined, I was under the impression that material possessions, money, cars, houses, and random women would fulfill that emptiness I so tried to cure. However, by being immature, I lacked spiritual awareness of being an eternal being. I kept trying to fulfill the spirit man with natural items, but that only led to an unregenerate state because the flesh's appetite was greater than the production of the fruit of the spirit. But Jesus Christ has bestowed His Shekinah Glory upon me, and that has transformed me back into His image. Now I am solely controlled by His divine influence called grace that produces holiness and righteousness.

This is not meant to chastise, but I got to ask: What are you filling yourself with? Most men only care for a woman's feelings, needs, and desires, but I care for your soul, which is my first obligation to you. I was both ecstatic and astounded when I received your missive and card. It was very beautiful and thoughtful. I apologize for the lack of communication on your birthday - Please charge it to my head and not my heart. There is not a day that passes, nor a sun that sets, that your name is not being expressed when I talk to my Daddy (Jesus).

Would it be fair to ask you what is the thought that comes to your mind when you think of me? A lot has transpired during our little semi-separation with me. That is mind-boggling to some. To others, it is inspiring.

Keep God first. Stay focused and steadfast on being this beautiful woman God created you to be. You can be that example of enlightenment for your son to identify who he was destined to be by the actions of a very dedicated, determined, disciplined, God-fearing woman he loves to see.

As I stated earlier, I just want to see you winning and to be saved. If you're successful, everyone around you and those attached to you will be saved and winning. That is equivalent to the plan God had for each of us from the beginning.

FROM LOKI TO QUINTON

TURNEY CENTER
2019

Dear self,

It has been a while since our last conversation, and I am so grateful - humbled even - that you set aside time to inquire about my well-being. A lot has transpired throughout your journey through prison, and I would like to take a second to remove the sunglasses of yesterday, prior to the forecast of today, amid uncertainty embracing what is yet to come.

I have analyzed and studied your beginning to your now. I studied how you have sabotaged, restored, and revived yourself through endless efforts of becoming and seeking your higher self. I have watched you destroy relationships with very loving and loyal women because of your manipulating tongue compounded with a radicalistic way of thinking. It became so obvious to them that you were seeking attachment over happiness in fear of loneliness. You were willing to risk the entire friendship because of selfish ambition.

I have observed how emotionally distraught you were, letting anger fester over unresolved issues that resulted in you physically lashing out at other people, particularly people whose image and struggles mirrored the issues you were battling with.

I heard conversations that you have partaken in - not because you were intrigued in the conversation, but simply lacking courage and fearing rejection. The thought of isolation triggered you to succumb to foolishness rather than igniting the higher self. For me, that defines the difference between ordinary and extraordinary. After the process of self-evaluation, I concluded you were very problematic, with a high level of dysfunction stemming from the demeanor you possessed. It came from traumatic events in prison, which opened the door to characteristics in total opposition to who God created you to be. It caused you to bypass the land called advancement, resulting in you wallowing in the field of mediocrity.

I chuckled privately as I observed you publicly eating scraps from the garden of pain. You overlooked the promotion of eating from the promise that awaits you in the palace of prosperity. During a close examination, I noticed a deep burning desire bubbling within your being to change the behavior that has been displayed, which can only be accomplished through rectifying your thinking.

Over time I sensed a spiritual awakening erupting in the depths of your soul that touched your spirit. It manifested throughout your entire being. I marveled at how you managed to restore healing to severely damaged lacerations through an enormous amount of patience and compassion. Honestly, I was astonished by your forgiveness and humility that paved the way to rebuilding bridges that were in unfathomable conditions, all because of the immaturity aroused from the kid more so than the maturity materializing from the king.

I was baffled by your sincere commitment to reviving yourself mentally through sleepless nights, studying various subjects, and self-striving vigorously to regain control of who you are rather than where you are. You focused on allowing who you have become to align with where you are going. I was overwhelmed by how passionate you were in pursuit of the peace of God, peace *in* God, and peace *with* God acquired by countless hours of studying, trusting, and believing His Word alongside consistent prayers. You prayed to resist the temptations of the world. Where I once saw you wandering into the spirit, I now see you living in it.

I am in utter disbelief to have witnessed a maturation process of a boy who lost his identity in the sea of his pleasures. But now, he is swimming upon his purpose in the ocean of opportunities. I am in a state of awe of how you have clothed yourself with love, joy, and peace when normally your outfit resembled hate, strife, and contempt. It is amazing to see how you respond to heavy opposition and hardships through the statues that have been embedded in you and light up your eyes. Your understanding produces a fruitful perception, which contrasts with the standards engraved in you that prohibited progression in any form. They were caused by the chains of simplicity and confusion you were so bound to. The fabric of your heart is now a symbol of hope that shines light upon those whose feet are stumbling down the path of darkness. They remain suffocated by the pressures of the creation as opposed to the freedom granted by the Creator. But as before, your heart was rough as a stone that guided men into dry places, drinking toxic water from the fountain of corruption tightly wrapped in the garment of destruction.

I am shocked by how extremely conscious you are of not defiling your temple. You didn't give into pleasures of the flesh like you used to. In the past, you were not fully aware of the purpose because of your hopes of satisfying the beast. No word in the dictionary can define the exuberance as I saw you leave the nest of comfort to spread your wings. You flew among foreign clouds resembling grace and mercy. You had the courage to land on the tree of life instead of crashing into the stoop of death.

REVELATION HAS TRANSFORMED ME BACK INTO THE IMAGE OF GOD instead of THE IMAGE OF THE WORLD...

WHEN I FOUND THE BOOK

TURNEY CENTER
2019

Journal Entry

Entangled within an environment unfamiliar to my nature, I was lost and confused. My mind became poisoned with hate, anger, and bitterness intertwined with resentment to the highest degree. Isolated while secluded, existing in a limited amount of space. After the years passed, my soul became weary from the fight as my spirit entered the final stages of war, numb from the bombardments of battle. I couldn't sleep, for my thoughts were constantly racing, synchronized with persistently pacing, causing deprivation due to the idle time spent on the pavement. Daily I was placed in a cage, handcuffed and shackled. At times I felt like an animal. At other times, an enslaved person. I was emotionally in bondage, constantly full of rage.

Vividly, I recall the memory of a woman who unknowingly changed the course of my life - exchanging my idleness, revealing my purpose with life's manual, and connecting it to a promise she knew not. I was skeptical for a moment, but really, I was afraid. I was even hesitant because of its powerful revelations and definitive content. I perceived the effects of reading the manuscript and how it could transform my consciousness. I started flirting with the writing on the pages, which led me to intimately date the chapters, experiencing love beyond human comprehension manifested by the totality of its message.

Studying the scrolls has increased my cognizance and intellect, removing the veil from my eyes to witness the two invisible governing powers at work in this world. I now realize that most are unaware of why they do the things they do and say what they say. They have no clue who is in control of what they say and the things they do. So, this book relegated a gift of understanding that is never the vessel, producing extraordinary insight as to who is in control of that vessel solely by the attitude, actions, and behavior exemplified by that vessel.

The historical cannons allow me to dissect my surroundings. It also allows me to identify that the mass majority is being controlled by the invisible governing power producing disobedience and rebellion. While a small majority of mankind is still in reverence to that invisible governing power that produces holiness and righteousness, it would be an understatement to say this book hasn't transformed my life. But it would also be an understatement to say this book would not change your life. This book has all the keys to success. This book is the Holy Bible. Would you like to be next?

TO THE WOMAN WHO INSPIRED ME

TURNEY CENTER
2019

Dear Mama,

A woman planted three seeds in the dark, rich soil of her love. Her spirit was embedded in the soil attached to her seeds, bringing light to the reflection of life. The strength in her tears watered the dry, harsh reality of previous generations. She lovingly pruned undesirable traits in hopes of producing morally upright fruit. She tirelessly pulled weeds of immaturity, unveiling her seed's identity. Upon daily inspection, the tenderness of her touch cultivated an environment engulfed in indescribable love, compassion, and persistence. The power of her pour instilled a high level of discipline and guidance, congruent with God's direction and purpose. The discomfort caused by her first harvest increased her awareness of the production of the second season. That perpetuated intense protection for the productivity of the third. The effect began an affectionate mentality displayed by unconventional behavior in the sight of onlookers. The youngest adopted an unmatched strength because of her smile, which shined like the sun despite numerous adversities and disadvantages.

Suffocating from the confined congestion of familiar seeds, she was feeding from the same pile of dirt. She transplanted herself to a new land of relationships and resources in hopes of flourishing into someone magnificent. Shortly after, she became conscious of the need for further growth. It was due to the limited opportunities to progress and thrive at the maximum capacity of her full potential. She surgically expanded her intellectual growth beyond the perimeter of her initial pot.

In time, she intertwined herself with the opposite creation to form a united covenant under God that the seeds only witnessed through the eyes of television. Now they both rest peacefully in the luxury of spiritual Eden, benefitting from hard work and dedication. No words can describe the beauty of the encompassing love of a mother. I am thankful and blessed God gave me the privilege to be a recipient of a queen who smothered her fear to capture her purpose.

CONCLUSION

During heavy opposition, I needed a channel to produce what I was thinking. Instead of allowing the mounting pressure of several murder charges to define me, writing became a tool that birthed a talent God buried inside me.

I never imagined my words impacting lives until I received inspiring feedback from the content of a letter I wrote. Daily, I pondered on the thought of a collection of letters to allow those on the inside and outside a firsthand peek into the depth of my mind. Nevertheless, I started expressing myself in ways I never deemed imaginable.

I began critically analyzing my surroundings while painting a picture with my words. My words described a picture illustrating a wide range of emotions intertwined with a high volume of frustrations, leading to the concept of developing *Incarcerated Thinking*.

As time passed, the writing mindset expanded from letters to topics dear to my heart. The more I wrote, the more my perspective changed as to why I wrote. At first,

I was writing hoping to challenge the reader to view my train of thought, which eventually altered to challenge the reader to examine *their* train of thought.

Despite facing harsh conditions coupled with multiple life sentences, I never allowed my situation to control how I think. I pray that *Incarcerated Thinking* inspires you to think beyond the demands that life will impose upon you.

IN MEMORY OF MY FRIEND & BROTHER

I dedicate this book to Kron Brown.
I'll never forget you Big Bruh!

July 31, 1982 – January 12, 2022